DOGS SET X

FRENCH BULLDOGS

Tamara L. Britton
ABDO Publishing Company

Published by ABDO Publishing Company, PO Box 398166, Minneapolis, MN 55439.
Copyright © 2013 by Abdo Consulting Group, Inc. International copyrights reserved
in all countries. No part of this book may be reproduced in any form without written
permission from the publisher. The Checkerboard Library™ is a trademark and logo of
ABDO Publishing Company.

Printed in the United States of America, North Mankato, Minnesota.
102012
012013

 PRINTED ON RECYCLED PAPER

Cover Photo: SuperStock
Interior Photos: Alamy p. 12; AP Images p. 19; iStockphoto pp. 9, 10–11, 15, 20–21;
      Thinkstock pp. 5, 7, 13, 16–17

Editors: Megan M. Gunderson, Stephanie Hedlund
Art Direction: Neil Klinepier

Cataloging-in-Publication Data

Britton, Tamara L., 1963-
 French bulldogs / Tamara L. Britton.
    p. cm. -- (Dogs)
 Includes bibliographical references and index.
 ISBN 978-1-61783-590-2
 1. French bulldog--Juvenile literature. 2. Dogs--Juvenile literature. I. Title.
636.72--dc23
               2012946332

CONTENTS

The Dog Family 4

French Bulldogs 6

What They're Like 8

Coat and Color. 10

Size 12

Care 14

Feeding 16

Things They Need 18

Puppies 20

Glossary 22

Web Sites. 23

Index 24

THE DOG FAMILY

Dogs come in many shapes, sizes, and personalities. There are more than 400 different **breeds**! All of these dogs belong to the family **Canidae**.

Dogs and humans have been living together for 12,000 years. All dogs descended from the gray wolf. Humans trained wolf pups to help them hunt. Over time, humans began breeding dogs for other activities.

One of these dogs is the French bulldog. It is a descendant of the English bulldog. Early English bulldogs were bred to be fighting dogs. But French bulldogs are just the opposite! These loving dogs were meant to be family companions. They are truly man's best friends!

The French bulldog

FRENCH BULLDOGS

In the late 1800s, workers in England began **breeding** smaller English bulldogs to be lapdogs. During the **Industrial Revolution**, many English workers moved to France. They took their little bulldogs with them.

In France, the bulldogs mated with other breeds. The puppies became known as the *Boule-Dog Français*, or French bulldog. These dogs became popular with wealthy families.

Americans visiting Paris brought French bulldog puppies home with them. In 1897, the French Bulldog Club of America was established. The following year, the **American Kennel Club (AKC)** recognized the breed.

Today, the French bulldog is the eighteenth most popular breed in the United States.

What They're Like

As companion dogs, French bulldogs are very affectionate. They love to be with their people! It is hard to resist their friendly manner.

These intelligent dogs are alert and curious. They can be good watchdogs. Frenchies do not bark often. But they can issue a warning bark if needed!

Though these cuddly dogs love to relax, they also enjoy an adventure. Playing outside and riding in the car are Frenchie favorites!

The French bulldog is in the AKC's non-sporting group. But that won't keep the fun-loving Frenchie from playing a little ball!

COAT AND COLOR

French bulldogs have short, smooth coats. Their fur can be black, **brindle**, **fawn**, cream, or white. Some Frenchie

Brindle and white

Black and white

10

coats have two of these colors. Others have one of these colors paired with white.

It is important to take care of your Frenchie's coat. It will need occasional brushing. More frequent brushing may be needed in spring and autumn. This is when Frenchies **shed**.

Black

Fawn

SIZE

French bulldogs should weigh less than 28 pounds (13 kg). Males usually weigh 24 to 28 pounds (11 to 13 kg). Females should weigh about 19 to 24 pounds (8 to 11 kg).

Short, stout legs support the Frenchie's well-rounded, muscular body and broad chest. Its head is half flat and half domed. The **breed**'s famous bat ears are broad at the base, round on the top, and stand erect.

Breeders carefully bred Frenchies so their ears would look like a bat's ears.

12

The **breed**'s short, broad **muzzle** has heavily wrinkled skin. This causes deep folds on the face. A black nose tips the dog's snout.

The Frenchie's short tail is either straight or screwed. It is thicker near the body and thinner at the tip.

Snore, snort, and wheeze! Those breathing noises you hear are caused by the Frenchie's short muzzle.

CARE

These active dogs like to go outside. But, French bulldogs are not outdoor dogs. They need to live inside where there is air conditioning.

Because of the shape of its face and **muzzle**, a French bulldog can have difficulty breathing. So, it can easily become overheated. You will need to watch your Frenchie's activity level. Do not let it get too hot.

Back problems and allergies are also common in this **breed**. So, regular visits with a veterinarian are important. Frenchies should also stay current with their **vaccines**. And, the veterinarian can **spay** or **neuter** your dog.

At home, check your Frenchie weekly for problems. A good time to do this is when the dog is groomed. Pay close attention to the skin folds on your Frenchie's face. They need to be kept clean and dry to avoid infection.

The Frenchie's short coat will not need frequent bathing. Let your nose be your guide!

FEEDING

French bulldogs need food that contains **protein**. Good dog food contains everything your dog needs. The three kinds of commercial dog foods are dry, semimoist, and canned. Each type offers different recipes based on age, weight, and health.

The food label will tell you how much to feed your dog and how often. Extra weight can strain its back. If you are concerned about your dog's weight, check with your veterinarian. He or she can recommend a healthy diet.

Be sure to wash your Frenchie's food dishes every day. Dogs also need plenty of fresh water. Make sure to have some available at all times!

Do not feed your dog too much! It can become overweight.

THINGS THEY NEED

Frenchies should be **socialized** and trained at an early age. Obedience training will teach them to be good canine citizens.

Your dog will need a leash, a collar, a license, and identification tags. Every Frenchie also needs sturdy food and water bowls, a soft bed, and some toys.

More than anything, French bulldogs need good, caring families. As companion dogs, they need attention. These loyal dogs will quickly bond with their owners.

Even if it has its own soft bed, your Frenchie may find your bed to be a nice substitute!

PUPPIES

Female French bulldogs are **pregnant** for about 63 days. On average, they give birth to four puppies. The tiny puppies are born blind and deaf.

The puppies see and hear when they are about 2 weeks old. At 3 weeks old, they will begin to explore their surroundings. They will begin to eat puppy food about one week later. When they are 12 to 16 weeks old, they are ready to be adopted.

Have you decided a French bulldog is a good fit for your family? If so, look for a well-known **breeder**. A good breeder tests his or her dogs for health problems.

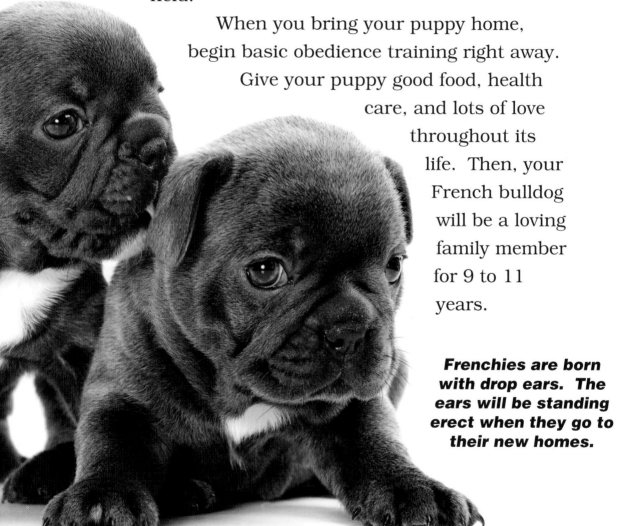

When choosing your pet, look for a playful, curious puppy. It should be willing to approach you and be held.

When you bring your puppy home, begin basic obedience training right away. Give your puppy good food, health care, and lots of love throughout its life. Then, your French bulldog will be a loving family member for 9 to 11 years.

Frenchies are born with drop ears. The ears will be standing erect when they go to their new homes.

GLOSSARY

American Kennel Club (AKC) - an organization that studies and promotes interest in purebred dogs.

breed - a group of animals sharing the same ancestors and appearance. A breeder is a person who raises animals. Raising animals is often called breeding them.

brindle - having dark streaks or spots on a gray, tan, or tawny background.

Canidae (KAN-uh-dee) - the scientific Latin name for the dog family. Members of this family are called canids. They include wolves, jackals, foxes, coyotes, and domestic dogs.

fawn - a light grayish brown color.

Industrial Revolution - a period in England from about 1750 to 1850. It marked the change from an agricultural to an industrial society.

muzzle - an animal's nose and jaws.

neuter (NOO-tuhr) - to remove a male animal's reproductive glands.

pregnant - having one or more babies growing within the body.

22

protein - a substance which provides energy to the body and serves as a major class of foods for animals. Foods high in protein include cheese, eggs, fish, meat, and milk.

shed - to cast off hair, feathers, skin, or other coverings or parts by a natural process.

socialize - to adapt an animal to behaving properly around people or other animals in various settings.

spay - to remove a female animal's reproductive organs.

vaccine (vak-SEEN) - a shot given to prevent illness or disease.

WEB SITES

To learn more about French bulldogs, visit ABDO Publishing Company online. Web sites about French bulldogs are featured on our Book Links page. These links are routinely monitored and updated to provide the most current information available.

www.abdopublishing.com

INDEX

A
adoption 20, 21
American Kennel Club
    6

B
bed 18
body 12, 13, 14, 16
breeder 6, 20

C
Canidae (family) 4
character 4, 8, 14, 18,
    21
coat 10, 11
collar 18
color 10, 11, 13

E
ears 12
England 6

F
face 13, 14, 15
food 16, 17, 18, 20, 21
France 6
French Bulldog Club of
    America 6

G
grooming 11, 15

H
head 12
health 14, 15, 16, 20,
    21
history 4, 6

L
leash 18
legs 12
license 18
life span 21

M
muzzle 13, 14

N
neuter 14
nose 13

P
puppies 6, 20, 21

R
reproduction 20

S
senses 20
shedding 11
size 12, 16
skin 13, 15
snout 13
socializing 18
spay 14

T
tail 13
toys 18
training 18, 21

U
United States 6

V
vaccines 14
veterinarian 14, 16

W
water 17, 18